LOCKPORT, ILLINOIS

1958 FORD EDSEL

LINCOLN LANDING

ILLINOIS
66

MW00807260

ILLINOIS

66

JOLIET AREA HISTORICAL MUSEUM
JOLIET, ILLINOIS

1942 CADILLAC

White Fence Farm

ILLINOIS
66

WHITE FENCE FARM RESTAURANT
ROMEOVILLE, ILLINOIS

1957 PACKARD

ILLINOIS
66

RESTORED STANDARD GAS STATION
ODELL, ILLINOIS

1932 DESOTO

Launching Pad

GEMINI GIANT

ILLINOIS
66

GEMINI GIANT
WILMINGTON, ILLINOIS

1956 CHEVY BEL AIR

COZY
DRIVE
IN
FOOD

COZY DOG DRIVE IN
SPRINGFIELD, ILLINOIS

1957 BUICK

ILLINOIS
66

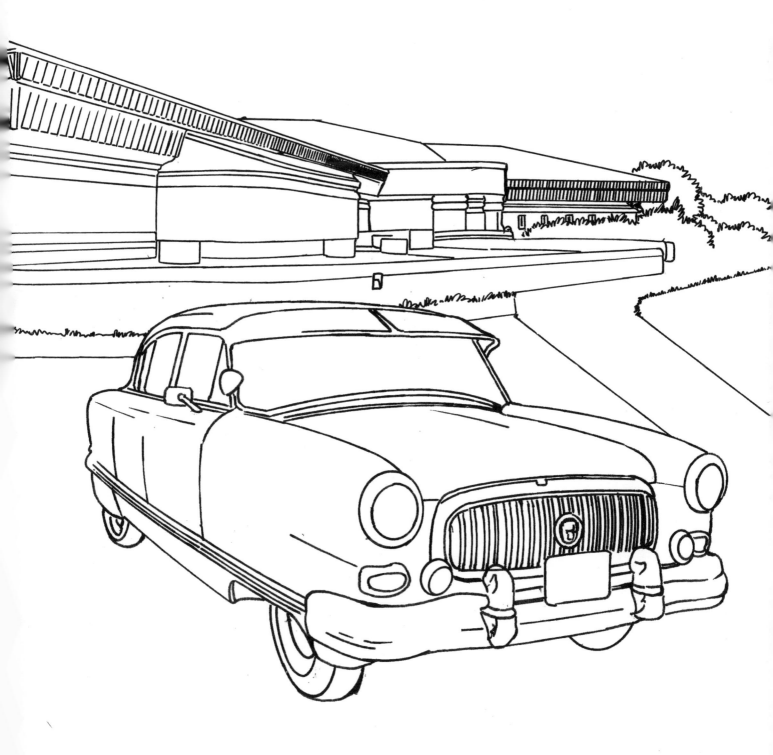

ILLINOIS
66

CAHOKIA MOUNDS HISTORIC SITE
COLLINSVILLE, ILLINOIS

1952 NASH

MISSOURI
66

GATEWAY ARCH
ST LOUIS, MISSOURI

1936 HUDSON

MERAMEC CAVERNS

CAVERNS

STANTON MO

MISSOURI
66

MERAMEC CAVERNS SIGN
STANTON, MISSOURI

1964 FORD GALAXIE

WAGON WHEEL MOTEL

MISSOURI 66

WAGON WHEEL MOTEL
CUBA, MISSOURI

1967 FORD MUSTANG

ROUTE 66 ROCKER

FANNING
US
66
OUTPOST

○ WORLD ○ ○ EST ○

MISSOURI
66

WORLD'S LARGEST ROCKING CHAIR
CUBA, MISSOURI

1948 NASH RAMBLER

KANSAS

66

MARSH ARCH BRIDGE
RIVERTON, KANSAS

1942 LASALLE

Bill Murphey's RESTAURANT

KANSAS
66

BILL MURPHEY'S RESTAURANT
BAXTER SPRINGS, KANSAS

1961 RAMBLER

ROUTE 66 PACKARD MUSEUM
AFTON, OKLAHOMA

1960 CORVETTE

OKLAHOMA

66

TULSA ROUTE 66

OKLAHOMA 66

ROUTE 66 GATEWAY
TULSA, OKLAHOMA

1956 FORD FAIRLANE

OKLAHOMA
66

BLUE WHALE
CATOOSA, OKLAHOMA

1938 FORD

ROUTE
U S
66

NATIONAL ROUTE 66 MUSEUM

OKLAHOMA
66

NATIONAL ROUTE 66 MUSEUM
ELK CITY, OKLAHOMA

1941 HUDSON

ARCADIA
ROUND
BARN

OKLAHOMA
66

ARCADIA ROUND BARN
ARCADIA, OKLAHOMA

1949 KAISER

the BIG TEXAN STEAK RANCH

TEXAS
66

BIG TEXAN STEAK RANCH SIGN
AMARILLO, TEXAS

1957 PLYMOUTH FURY

TEXAS
66

RESTORED PHILLIPS 66 GAS STATION
MCLEAN, TEXAS

1951 FORD F100

TEXAS
66

CADILLAC RANCH
AMARILLO, TEXAS

1956 CHEVY BEL AIR

TEXAS
66

U DROP INN
SHAMROCK, TEXAS

1949 PACKARD

U.S. AIR FORCE
Kirtland Air Force Base

NEW MEXICO
66

AIR SHOW AT KIRTLAND AFB
ALBUQUERQUE, NEW MEXICO

1955 HUDSON

INDIAN
PUEBLO
CULTURAL
CENTER

NEW MEXICO
66

INDIAN PUEBLO CULTURAL CENTER
ALBUQUERQUE NEW MEXICO

1955 DESOTO

BLUE SWALLOW MOTEL
TUCUMCARI, NEW MEXICO

1953 BUICK

NEW MEXICO

66

MINING MUSEUM

GO UNDERGROUND

NEW MEXICO
66

NEW MEXICO MINING MUSEUM
GRANTS, NEW MEXICO

1936 PACKARD

NEW MEXICO

66

MISSION OF SAN MIGUEL
SANTA FE, NEW MEXICO

1947 HUDSON

NEW MEXICO

66

RED ROCK BALLOON RALLY
GALLUP, NEW MEXICO

1942 CADILLAC

NEW MEXICO

66

HOTEL EL RANCHO
GALLUP, NEW MEXICO

1960 CADILLAC

GIANT ARROW LANDMARKS
TWIN ARROWS, ARIZONA

1952 HUDSON

ARIZONA
66

ARIZONA
66

WIGWAM VILLAGE MOTEL
HOLBROOK, ARIZONA

1952 BUICK

ARIZONA
66

OLD WEST MINING TOWN
OATMAN, ARIZONA

1949 KAISER

ARIZONA
66

GRAND CANYON RAILWAY HOTEL
WILLIAMS, ARIZONA

1953 MERCURY

AZTEC HOTEL

HOTELS

CALIFORNIA

66

AZTEC HOTEL
MONROVIA, CALIFORNIA

1952 OLDSMOBILE

NEEDLES
CALIFORNIA

CALIFORNIA
66

AUTHENTIC 19TH CENTURY WAGON
NEEDLES, CALIFORNIA

1968 MERCURY

SANTA MONICA PIER
SANTA MONICA, CALIFORNIA

1957 DESOTO

CALIFORNIA
66